Slow Cooker MAGIC

Publications International, Ltd.

Favorite Brand Name Recipes at www.fbnr.com

Front cover photography by Sanders Studios, Inc.

Pictured on the front cover: Vegetarian Chili *(page 60)*.

Pictured on the back cover *(top to bottom):* Triple Delicious Hot Chocolate *(page 86),* Mediterranean Red Potatoes *(page 76)* and Mu Shu Turkey *(page 46)*.

ISBN: 0-7853-5428-X

Manufactured in China.

8 7 6 5 4 3 2 1

Nutritional Analysis: Nutritional information is given for some of the recipes in this publication. Each analysis is based on the food items in the ingredient list, except ingredients labeled as "optional" or "for garnish." When more than one ingredient choice is listed, the first ingredient is used for analysis. If a range for the amount of an ingredient is given, the nutritional analysis is based on the lowest amount. Foods offered as "serve with" suggestions are not included in the analysis unless otherwise stated.

Microwave Cooking: Microwave ovens vary in wattage. Use the cooking times as guidelines and check for doneness before adding more time.

Slow Cooker
RECIPES

INTRODUCTION

Join the countless number of people who have discovered just how delicious mealtime can be with the help of the slow cooker. As you leave for work or play, turn the slow cooker on, and upon your return a hot and hearty meal awaits you. The days of carry-out food and frozen dinners are finally over. The slow cooker is truly the no-fuss way to prepare dinner.

Read through the following tips to learn more about this time-tested kitchen appliance.

THE BENEFITS

- No need for constant attention or frequent stirring

- No worry about burning or overcooking

- No sink full of pots and pans to scrub at the end of a long day

- Great for parties and buffets

- Keeps your kitchen cool by keeping your oven turned off

- Saves energy—cooking on the low setting uses less energy than most light bulbs

• As with conventional cooking recipes, slow cooker recipe time ranges are provided to account for variables such as temperature of ingredients before cooking, how full the slow cooker is and even altitude. Once you become familiar with your slow cooker you'll have a good idea which end of the range to use.

• Manufacturers recommend that slow cookers should be one-half to three-quarters full for best results.

• Keep a lid on it! The slow cooker can take as long as twenty minutes to regain the heat lost when the cover is removed. If the recipe calls for stirring or checking the dish near the end of the cooking time, replace the lid as quickly as you can.

• Save money and gain flavor by choosing tougher inexpensive cuts of meat for use with slow cooker recipes. The long cooking times help break down the toughness of the meat.

• Chicken skin tends to shrivel and curl in the slow cooker, so most recipes call for skinless chicken. If you prefer skin-on pieces, brown them in a skillet before adding them to the slow cooker.

• To clean your slow cooker, follow the manufacturer's instructions. To make cleanup even easier, spray with nonstick cooking spray before adding food.

• Always taste the finished dish before serving and adjust seasonings to your preference. Consider adding a dash of any of the following: salt, pepper, seasoned salt, seasoned herb blends, lemon juice, soy sauce, Worcestershire sauce, flavored vinegar, freshly ground pepper or minced fresh herbs.

To easily lift a dish or a meatloaf out of the slow cooker, make foil handles according to the following directions.

Tear off three 18×3-inch strips of heavy-duty foil. Crisscross the strips so they resemble the spokes of a wheel. Place your dish or food in the center of the strips.

Pull the foil strips up and over and place into the slow cooker. Leave them in while you cook so you can easily lift the item out again when ready.

Your best weapon against food contamination is organization. A clean and organized kitchen is a happy kitchen.

Read the entire recipe before you begin to be sure you have all the necessary ingredients and utensils required.

It is a good idea to have two cutting boards on hand. Use one for cutting raw meat, poultry and fish and the other for cutting fresh fruits, vegetables and other foods. Always wash cutting boards and utensils with hot soapy water after each use.

If you do any advance preparation, such as trimming meat or cutting vegetables, refrigerate the food until you're ready to start cooking. Store food in resealable plastic food storage bags. To avoid cross contamination, always place raw meat, poultry and fish on the lowest shelf in the refrigerator. Place fruits and  vegetables on higher shelves or in a crisper drawer. Once your dish is cooked, don't keep it in the slow cooker too long. Foods need to be kept cooler than 40°F or hotter than 140°F to avoid the growth of harmful bacteria. Remove food to a clean container, cover and refrigerate as soon as possible. Do not reheat leftovers in the slow cooker. Use a microwave oven, the range-top or the oven for reheating.

By following these simple techniques and using the exciting recipes in this publication, you will soon be preparing wonderful dishes with minimal effort.

SOUP'S ON

Rustic Vegetable Soup

1 jar (16 ounces) picante sauce
1 package (10 ounces) frozen mixed vegetables,
    thawed
1 package (10 ounces) frozen cut green beans,
    thawed
1 can (10 ounces) condensed beef broth, undiluted
1 to 2 baking potatoes, cut in ½-inch pieces
1 medium green bell pepper, chopped
½ teaspoon sugar
¼ cup finely chopped parsley

Combine all ingredients, except parsley, in slow cooker.
Cover and cook on LOW 8 hours or on HIGH 4 hours.
Stir in parsley; serve. *Makes 8 servings*

Farmhouse Ham and Vegetable Chowder

2 cans (10½ ounces each) cream of celery soup
2 cups diced cooked ham
1 package (10 ounces) frozen corn
1 large baking potato, cut in ½-inch pieces
1 medium red bell pepper, diced
½ teaspoon dried thyme leaves
2 cups small broccoli florets
½ cup milk

1. Combine all ingredients, except broccoli and milk in slow cooker; stir to blend. Cover and cook on LOW 6 to 8 hours or on HIGH 3 to 4 hours.

2. If cooking on LOW, turn to HIGH and stir in broccoli and milk. Cover and cook 15 minutes or until broccoli is crisp tender.   *Makes 6 servings*

Farmhouse Ham and Vegetable Chowder

Easy Italian Vegetable Soup

1 can (14½ ounces) diced tomatoes, undrained
1 can (10½ ounces) condensed beef broth, undiluted
1 package (8 ounces) sliced mushrooms
1 medium zucchini, thinly sliced
1 medium green bell pepper, chopped
1 medium yellow onion, chopped
⅓ cup dry red wine or beef broth
1½ tablespoons dried basil leaves
2½ teaspoons sugar
1 tablespoon extra virgin olive oil
½ teaspoon salt
1 cup (4 ounces) shredded Mozzarella cheese
    (optional)

1. Combine tomatoes, broth, mushrooms, zucchini, bell pepper, onion, wine, basil and sugar in slow cooker. Cook on LOW 8 hours or on HIGH 4 hours.

2. Stir oil and salt into soup. Garnish with cheese, if desired.   *Makes 5 to 6 servings*

Ham and Navy Bean Soup

8 ounces dried navy beans, rinsed and drained
6 cups water
1 ham bone
1 medium yellow onion, chopped
2 celery stalks, finely chopped
2 bay leaves
1½ teaspoons dried tarragon leaves
1½ teaspoons salt
¼ teaspoon black pepper

1. Place beans in large bowl; cover completely with water. Soak 6 to 8 hours or overnight. Drain beans; discard water.

2. Combine beans, water, ham bone, onion, celery, bay leaves and tarragon leaves in slow cooker. Cook on LOW 8 hours or on HIGH 4 hours. Discard ham bone and bay leaves; stir in salt and pepper.

Makes 8 servings

Double Thick Baked Potato-Cheese Soup

    2 pounds baking potatoes, peeled and cut into
       ½-inch cubes
    2 cans (10½ ounces each) cream of mushroom soup
1½ cups finely chopped green onions, divided
    ¼ teaspoon garlic powder
    ⅛ teaspoon ground red pepper
1½ cups (6 ounces) shredded sharp Cheddar cheese
    1 cup (8 ounces) sour cream
    1 cup milk
    Black pepper

1. Combine potatoes, soup, 1 cup green onions, garlic powder and red pepper in slow cooker. Cover and cook on LOW 8 hours or on HIGH 4 hours.

2. Add cheese, sour cream and milk; stir until cheese has completely melted. Cover and cook on HIGH an additional 10 minutes. Season to taste with black pepper. Garnish with remaining green onions.

Makes 7 Servings

Creamy Turkey Soup

2 cans (10½ ounces each) cream of chicken soup
2 cups chopped cooked turkey breast meat
1 package (8 ounces) sliced mushrooms
1 medium yellow onion, chopped
1 teaspoon rubbed sage *or* ½ teaspoon dried poultry
   seasoning
1 cup frozen peas, thawed
½ cup milk
1 jar (about 4 ounces) diced pimiento

1. Combine soup, turkey, mushrooms, onion and sage in slow cooker. Cook on LOW 8 hours or on HIGH 4 hours.

2. If cooking on LOW, turn to HIGH; stir in peas, milk and pimientos. Cook an additional 10 minutes or until heated through.

Makes 5 to 6 servings

Creamy Turkey Soup

Campfire Sausage and Potato Soup

1 can (15½ ounces) dark kidney beans, rinsed and
    drained
1 can (14½ ounces) diced tomatoes, undrained
1 can (10½ ounces) condensed beef broth, undiluted
8 ounces kielbasa sausage, cut lengthwise into
    halves, then crosswise into ½-inch pieces
1 large baking potato, cut into ½-inch cubes
1 medium green bell pepper, diced
1 medium onion, diced
1 teaspoon dried oregano leaves
½ teaspoon sugar
1 to 2 teaspoons ground cumin

Combine all ingredients, except cumin, in slow cooker.
Cover and cook on LOW 8 hours or on HIGH 4 hours.
Stir in cumin; serve.   *Makes 6 to 7 servings*

HELPFUL HINT

Kielbasa sausage,
also referred to as
Polish sausage, is
sold both fresh and in
precooked links near the deli
aisle.

*Campfire Sausage and
Potato Soup*

MAIN-DISH MAGIC

Caribbean Shrimp with Rice

1 package (12 ounces) frozen shrimp, thawed
½ cup chicken broth
1 clove garlic, minced
1 teaspoon chili powder
½ teaspoon salt
½ teaspoon dried oregano leaves
1 cup frozen peas
½ cup diced tomatoes
2 cups cooked rice

Combine shrimp, broth, garlic, chili powder, salt and oregano in slow cooker. Cover and cook on LOW 2 hours. Add peas and tomatoes. Cover and cook on LOW 5 minutes. Stir in rice. Cover and cook on LOW an additional 5 minutes. *Makes 4 servings*

Sweet and Sour Spare Ribs

    4 pounds spare ribs
    2 cups dry sherry or chicken broth
    ½ cup pineapple, mango or guava juice
    ⅓ cup chicken broth
    1 clove garlic, minced
    2 tablespoons brown sugar
    2 tablespoons cider vinegar
    2 tablespoons soy sauce
    ½ teaspoon salt
    ¼ teaspoon black pepper
    ⅛ teaspoon red pepper flakes
    1 tablespoon cornstarch

1. Preheat oven to 400°F. Place ribs in foil-lined shallow roasting pan. Bake 30 minutes, turning over after 15 minutes. Remove from oven. Slice meat into 2-rib portions. Place ribs in 5-quart slow cooker. Add remaining ingredients, except cornstarch, to slow cooker.

2. Cover and cook on LOW 6 hours. Uncover and skim fat from liquid.

3. Combine cornstarch and ¼ cup liquid from slow cooker; stir until smooth. Pour mixture back into slow cooker; mix well. Cover and cook on HIGH 10 minutes or until slightly thickened.   *Makes 4 servings*

Sweet and Sour Spare Ribs

Shredded Pork Wraps

1 cup salsa, divided
2 tablespoons cornstarch
1 bone-in pork sirloin roast (2 pounds)
6 (8-inch) flour tortillas
⅓ cup shredded reduced-fat Cheddar cheese
3 cups broccoli slaw mix

1. Combine ¼ cup salsa and cornstarch in small bowl; stir until smooth. Pour mixture into slow cooker. Top with pork roast. Pour remaining ¾ cup salsa over roast.

2. Cover and cook on LOW 6 to 8 hours or until internal temperature reaches 165°F when tested with meat thermometer inserted into the thickest part of roast, not touching bone. Remove roast from slow cooker. Transfer roast to cutting board; cover with foil and let stand 10 to 15 minutes or until cool enough to handle before shredding. Internal temperature will rise 5° to 10°F during stand time. Trim and discard outer fat from pork. Using 2 forks, pull pork into coarse shreds.

3. Divide shredded meat evenly on each tortilla. Spoon about 2 tablespoons salsa mixture on top of meat in each tortilla. Top evenly with cheese and broccoli slaw mix. Fold bottom edge of tortilla over filling; fold in sides. Roll up completely to enclose filling. Repeat with remaining tortillas. Serve remaining salsa mixture as a dipping sauce.

Makes 6 servings

Shredded Pork Wrap

Corned Beef and Cabbage

1 head cabbage (1½ pounds), cut into 6 wedges
4 ounces baby carrots
1 corned beef (3-pounds) with seasoning packet*
⅓ cup prepared mustard (optional)
⅓ cup honey (optional)

*If seasoning packet is not perforated, poke several small holes with tip of paring knife.

1. Place cabbage in slow cooker; top with carrots.

2. Place seasoning packet on top of vegetables. Place corned beef fat side up over seasoning packet and vegetables. Add 1 quart water. Cover and cook on LOW 10 hours.

3. Discard seasoning packet. Just before serving, combine mustard and honey in small bowl. Use as dipping sauce, if desired.   *Makes 6 servings*

Corned Beef and Cabbage

Chicken Teriyaki

1 pound boneless skinless chicken tenders
1 can (6 ounces) pineapple juice
¼ cup soy sauce
1 tablespoon sugar
1 tablespoon minced fresh ginger
1 tablespoon minced garlic
1 tablespoon vegetable oil
1 tablespoon molasses
24 cherry tomatoes (optional)
2 cups hot cooked rice

Combine all ingredients, except rice, in slow cooker.
Cover and cook on LOW 2 hours. Serve chicken and
sauce over rice.   *Makes 4 servings*

HELPFUL HINT

Chicken "tenders"
or "supremes" are
lean, tender strips
found on the underside
of the breast.

Southwestern Turkey in Chilies and Cream

1 boneless skinless turkey breast, cut into 1-inch
     pieces
2 tablespoons plus 2 teaspoons flour, divided
1 can (15 ounces) corn, well drained
1 can (4 ounces) diced green chilies, well drained
1 tablespoon butter
½ cup chicken broth
1 clove garlic, minced
1 teaspoon salt
½ teaspoon paprika
¼ teaspoon dried oregano leaves
¼ teaspoon black pepper
½ cup heavy cream
2 tablespoons chopped cilantro
3 cups hot cooked rice or pasta

1. Coat turkey pieces with 2 tablespoons flour; set aside.
Place corn and green chilies in slow cooker.

2. Melt butter in large nonstick skillet over medium
heat. Add turkey pieces; cook and stir 5 minutes or until
lightly browned. Place turkey in slow cooker. Add broth,
garlic, salt, paprika, oregano and pepper. Cover and cook
on LOW 2 hours.

3. Stir cream and remaining 2 teaspoons flour in small
bowl until smooth. Pour mixture into slow cooker. Cover
and cook on HIGH 10 minutes or until slightly
thickened. Stir in cilantro. Serve over rice.

Makes 6 (1½-cups) servings

Broccoli & Cheese Strata

 2 cups chopped broccoli florets
 4 slices firm white bread, ½-inch thick
 4 teaspoons butter
1½ cups (6 ounces) shredded Cheddar cheese
 3 eggs
1½ cups reduced-fat (2%) milk
 ½ teaspoon salt
 ½ teaspoon hot pepper sauce
 ⅛ teaspoon black pepper

1. Cook broccoli in boiling water 10 minutes or until tender. Drain. Spread one side of each bread slice with 1 teaspoon butter.

2. Arrange 2 slices bread, buttered sides up in greased 1-quart casserole. Layer cheese, broccoli and remaining 2 bread slices, buttered sides down.

3. Beat together eggs, milk, salt, hot pepper sauce and pepper in medium bowl. Gradually pour over bread.

4. Place small wire rack in 5-quart slow cooker. Pour in 1 cup water. Place casserole on rack. Cover and cook on HIGH 3 hours.   *Makes 4 servings*

Broccoli & Cheese Strata

Beef and Vegetables in Rich Burgundy Sauce

1 package (8 ounces) sliced mushrooms
1 package (8 ounces) baby carrots
1 medium green bell pepper, cut into thin strips
1 boneless chuck roast (2½ pounds)
1 can (10½ ounces) golden mushroom soup
¼ cup dry red wine or beef broth
1 tablespoon Worcestershire sauce
1 package (1 ounce) dried onion soup mix
¼ teaspoon black pepper
2 tablespoons water
3 tablespoons cornstarch
4 cups hot cooked noodles
   Chopped fresh parsley (optional)

1. Place mushrooms, carrots and bell pepper in slow cooker. Place roast on top of vegetables. Combine soup, wine, Worcestershire sauce, soup mix and black pepper in medium bowl; mix well. Pour soup mixture over roast. Cover and cook on LOW 8 to 10 hours.

2. Blend water into cornstarch in cup until smooth; set aside. Transfer roast to cutting board; cover with foil. Let stand 10 to 15 minutes before slicing.

3. Turn slow cooker to HIGH. Stir cornstarch mixture into vegetable mixture; cover and cook 10 minutes or until thickened. Serve over cooked noodles. Garnish with parsley, if desired.   *Makes 6 to 8 servings*

*Beef and Vegetables in
Rank Burgundy Sauce*

Country Captain Chicken

4 chicken thighs
2 tablespoons all-purpose flour
2 tablespoons vegetable oil, divided
1 cup chopped green bell pepper
1 large onion, chopped
1 celery stalk, chopped
1 clove garlic, minced
¼ cup chicken broth
2 cups canned or fresh crushed tomatoes
½ cup golden raisins
1½ teaspoons curry powder
1 teaspoon salt
¼ teaspoon paprika
¼ teaspoon black pepper
2 cups hot cooked rice

1. Coat chicken with flour; set aside. Heat 1 tablespoon oil in large skillet over medium-high heat until hot. Add bell pepper, onion, celery and garlic. Cook and stir 5 minutes or until vegetables are tender. Place vegetables in slow cooker.

2. Heat remaining tablespoon oil in same skillet over medium-high heat. Add chicken and cook 5 minutes per side. Place chicken in slow cooker.

3. Pour broth into skillet. Heat over medium-high heat, stirring frequently and scraping up any browned bits from bottom of skillet. Pour liquid into slow cooker. Add tomatoes, raisins, curry powder, salt, paprika and pepper. Cover and cook on LOW 3 hours. Serve chicken with sauce over rice. *Makes 4 servings*

Mama Mia Spaghetti Sauce

1 tablespoon olive oil
1 package (8 ounces) sliced mushrooms
½ cup finely chopped carrots
1 clove garlic, minced
1 shallot, minced
1 pound lean ground beef
2 cups canned or fresh crushed tomatoes
½ cup dry red wine or beef broth
2 tablespoons tomato paste
1 teaspoon salt
1 teaspoon dried oregano leaves
½ teaspoon dried basil leaves
¼ teaspoon black pepper
4 cups cooked spaghetti
Grated Parmesan cheese (optional)

1. Heat oil in large skillet over medium-high heat until hot. Add mushrooms, carrots, garlic and shallot to skillet. Cook and stir 5 minutes.

2. Place vegetables in slow cooker. Stir in ground beef crumbling it with spoon. Stir in tomatoes, wine, tomato paste, salt, oregano, basil and pepper. Cover and cook on HIGH 3 to 4 hours. Serve sauce with cooked spaghetti. Sprinkle with Parmesan cheese, if desired.

Makes 5 servings

De-Lite-Ful Dinners

& Desserts

Sweet Chicken Curry

   1 pound boneless skinless chicken breast, cut into
      1-inch pieces
   1 large green or red bell pepper, cut into 1-inch
      pieces
   1 large onion, sliced
   1 large tomato, seeded and chopped
   ½ cup mango chutney
   2 tablespoons cornstarch
1½ teaspoons curry powder
1⅓ cups hot cooked rice

1. Place chicken, bell pepper and onion in slow cooker. Top with tomato. Mix chutney, ¼ cup water, cornstarch and curry powder in large bowl.

continued on page 40

38

Sweet Curry Chicken, *continued*

2. Pour chutney mixture over chicken mixture in slow cooker. Cover and cook on LOW 3½ to 4½ hours. Serve over rice. *Makes 4 servings*

Nutrients per serving: *Calories: 326, Calories from Fat: 9%, Protein: 28 g, Carbohydrate: 45 g, Cholesterol: 69 mg, Sodium: 73 mg, Fiber: 3 g*
DIETARY EXCHANGES: *1 Vegetable, 1 Fruit, 1 Starch, 3 Lean Meat*

Hungarian Lamb Goulash

    1 package (16 ounces) frozen cut green beans
    1 cup chopped onion
1¼ pounds lean lamb stew meat, cut into 1-inch pieces
    1 can (15 ounces) chunky tomato sauce
1¾ cups reduced-sodium chicken broth
    1 can (6 ounces) tomato paste
    4 teaspoons paprika
    3 cups hot cooked noodles

Place green beans and onion in slow cooker. Top with lamb. Combine remaining ingredients, except noodles in large bowl; mix well. Pour over lamb mixture. Cover and cook on LOW 6 to 8 hours. Stir. Serve over noodles. *Makes 6 servings*

Nutrients per serving: *Calories: 289, Calories from Fat: 16%, Protein: 22 g, Carbohydrate: 39 g, Cholesterol: 67 mg, Sodium: 772 mg, Fiber: 7 g*
DIETARY EXCHANGES: *2 Vegetable, 2 Starch, 2 Lean Meat*

Orange Teriyaki Pork

Nonstick cooking spray
1 pound lean pork stew meat, cut into 1-inch cubes
1 package (16 ounces) frozen pepper blend for
    stir-fry
4 ounces sliced water chestnuts
½ cup orange juice
2 tablespoons quick-cooking tapioca
2 tablespoons brown sugar
2 tablespoons teriyaki sauce
½ teaspoon ground ginger
½ teaspoon dry mustard
1⅓ cups hot cooked rice

1. Spray large nonstick skillet with cooking spray; heat over medium heat until hot. Add pork; brown on all sides. Remove from heat; set aside.

2. Place peppers and water chestnuts in slow cooker. Top with browned pork. Mix orange juice, tapioca, brown sugar, teriyaki sauce, ginger and mustard in large bowl. Pour over pork mixture in slow cooker. Cover and cook on LOW 3 to 4 hours. Stir. Serve over rice.

Makes 4 servings

Nutrients per serving: *Calories: 313, Calories from Fat: 18%, Protein: 21 g, Carbohydrate: 42 g, Cholesterol: 49 mg, Sodium: 406 mg, Fiber: 4 g*
DIETARY EXCHANGES: *2 Vegetable, 2 Starch, 2 Lean Meat*

Hearty Lentil Stew

1 cup dried lentils, rinsed and drained
1 package (16 ounces) frozen green beans
2 cups cauliflower florets
1 cup chopped onion
1 cup baby carrots, cut in half crosswise
3 cups fat free reduced-sodium chicken broth
2 teaspoons ground cumin
¾ teaspoon ground ginger
1 can (15 ounces) chunky tomato sauce with garlic
   and herbs
½ cup dry-roasted peanuts

1. Place lentils in slow cooker. Top with green beans, cauliflower, onion and carrots. Combine broth, cumin and ginger in large bowl; mix well. Pour mixture over vegetables. Cover and cook on LOW 9 to 11 hours.

2. Stir in tomato sauce. Cover and cook on LOW 10 minutes. Ladle stew into bowls. Sprinkle peanuts evenly onto each serving.   *Makes 6 servings*

Nutrients per serving: *Calories: 264, Calories from Fat: 22%, Protein: 19 g, Carbohydrate: 35 g, Cholesterol: 0 mg, Sodium: 667 mg, Fiber: 16 g*
DIETARY EXCHANGES: *1 Vegetable, 2 Starch, 1 Lean Meat, 1 Fat*

Hearty Lentil Stew

Pork and Mushroom Ragout

   Nonstick cooking spray
 1 boneless pork loin roast (1¼ pounds)
1¼ cups canned crushed tomatoes, divided
 2 tablespoons cornstarch
 2 teaspoons dried savory leaves
 3 sun-dried tomatoes, patted dry and chopped
 1 package (8 ounces) sliced mushrooms
 1 large onion, sliced
 1 teaspoon black pepper
 3 cups hot cooked noodles

1. Spray large nonstick skillet with cooking spray; heat over medium heat until hot. Brown roast on all sides; set aside.

2. Combine ½ cup crushed tomatoes, cornstarch, savory and sun-dried tomatoes in large bowl. Pour mixture into slow cooker. Layer mushrooms, onion and roast over tomato mixture.

3. Pour remaining tomatoes over roast; sprinkle with pepper. Cover and cook on LOW 4 to 6 hours or until internal temperature reaches 165°F when tested with meat thermometer inserted into the thickest part of roast.

continued on page 46

Pork and Mushroom Ragout

Pork and Mushroom Ragout, *continued*

4. Remove roast from slow cooker. Transfer roast to cutting board; cover with foil. Let stand 10 to 15 minutes before slicing. Internal temperature will continue to rise 5° to 10°F during stand time. Serve over hot cooked noodles. *Makes 6 servings.*

Nutrients per serving: *Calories: 275, Calories from Fat: 22%, Protein: 21 g, Carbohydrate: 33 g, Cholesterol: 68 mg, Sodium: 169 mg, Fiber: 3 g*
DIETARY EXCHANGES: *1 Vegetable, 2 Starch, 2 Lean Meat*

Sweet Jalapeño Mustard Turkey Thighs

 3 **turkey thighs, skin removed**
¾ **cup honey mustard**
½ **cup orange juice**
 1 **tablespoon cider vinegar**
 1 **teaspoon Worcestershire sauce**
 1 to 2 **jalapeño peppers, finely chopped**
 1 **clove garlic, minced**
½ **teaspoon grated orange peel**

Place turkey thighs in single layer in slow cooker. Combine remaining ingredients in large bowl. Pour mixture over turkey thighs. Cover and cook on LOW 5 to 6 hours. *Makes 6 servings*

Nutrients per serving: Calories: 157, Calories from Fat: 22%, Protein: 14 g, Carbohydrate: 14 g, Cholesterol: 40 mg, Sodium: 92 mg, Fiber: 1 g
DIETARY EXCHANGES: 1 Fruit, 1 Lean Meat

Irish Stew

1 cup fat-free reduced-sodium chicken broth

1 teaspoon dried marjoram leaves

1 teaspoon dried parsley leaves

¾ teaspoon salt

½ teaspoon garlic powder

¼ teaspoon black pepper

1¼ pounds white potatoes, peeled and cut into 1-inch pieces

1 pound lean lamb stew meat, cut into 1-inch cubes

8 ounces frozen cut green beans

2 small leeks, cut lengthwise into halves then crosswise into slices

1½ cups coarsely chopped carrots

Combine broth, marjoram, parsley, salt, garlic powder and pepper in large bowl; mix well. Pour mixture into slow cooker. Add potatoes, lamb, green beans, leeks and carrots. Cover and cook on LOW for 7 to 9 hours.

Makes 6 servings

Nutrients per serving: *Calories: 256, Calories from Fat: 20%, Protein: 20 g, Carbohydrate: 32 g, Cholesterol: 52 mg, Sodium: 388 mg, Fiber: 5 g*
DIETARY EXCHANGES: *2 Vegetable, 2 Starch, 2 Lean Meat*

Mu Shu Turkey

   1 can (16 ounces) plums, drained, rinsed and pitted
½ cup orange juice
¼ cup finely chopped onion
   1 tablespoon minced fresh ginger
¼ teaspoon ground cinnamon
   1 pound boneless turkey breast, cut into thin strips
   6 (7-inch) flour tortillas
   3 cups coleslaw mix

1. Place plums in blender or food processor. Cover and blend until almost smooth. Combine plums, orange juice, onion, ginger and cinnamon in slow cooker; mix well. Place turkey strips over plum mixture. Cover and cook on LOW 3 to 4 hours.

2. Remove turkey strips from slow cooker and divide evenly among the tortillas. Spoon about 2 tablespoons plum sauce over turkey. Top evenly with coleslaw mix. Fold bottom edge of tortilla over filling; fold in sides. Roll up to completely enclose filling. Repeat with remaining tortillas. Use remaining plum sauce for dipping.

Makes 6 servings

Nutrients per serving: *Calories: 248, Calories from Fat: 14%, Protein: 17 g, Carbohydrate: 36 g, Cholesterol: 30 mg, Sodium: 282 mg, Fiber: 3 g*
DIETARY EXCHANGES: *1 Vegetable, 1 Fruit, 1 Starch, 2 Lean Meat*

Mu Shu Turkey

Sauerbraten

        1 boneless, beef sirloin tip roast (1¼ pounds)
        3 cups baby carrots
    1½ cups fresh or frozen pearl onions
        ¼ cup raisins
        ½ cup water
        ½ cup red wine vinegar
        1 tablespoon honey
        ½ teaspoon salt
        ½ teaspoon dry mustard
        ½ teaspoon garlic-pepper seasoning
        ¼ teaspoon ground cloves
        ¼ cup crushed crisp gingersnap cookies (5 cookies)

1. Heat large nonstick skillet over medium heat until hot. Brown roast on all sides; set aside.

2. Place roast, carrots, onions and raisins in slow cooker. Combine water, vinegar, honey, salt, mustard, garlic-pepper seasoning and cloves in large bowl; mix well. Pour mixture over meat and vegetables.

3. Cover and cook on LOW 4 to 6 hours or until internal temperature reaches 145°F when tested with meat thermometer inserted into thickest part of roast. Transfer roast to cutting board; cover with foil. Let stand 10 to 15 minutes before slicing. Internal temperature will continue to rise 5° to 10°F during stand time.

continued on page 52

Sauerbraten

Sauerbraten, *continued*

4. Remove vegetables with slotted spoon to bowl; cover to keep warm. Stir crushed cookies into sauce mixture in slow cooker. Cover and cook on HIGH 10 to 15 minutes or until sauce thickens. Serve meat and vegetables with sauce. *Makes 5 servings*

Nutrients per serving: *Calories: 296, Calories from Fat: 26%, Protein: 28 g, Carbohydrate: 25 g, Cholesterol: 57 mg, Sodium: 381 mg, Fiber: 4 g*
DIETARY EXCHANGES: *3 Vegetable, 1 Fruit, 1 Starch, 3 Lean Meat*

Pear Crunch

  1 can (8 ounces) crushed pineapple in juice, undrained
  ¼ cup pineapple or apple juice
  3 tablespoons dried cranberries
1½ teaspoons quick-cooking tapioca
  ¼ teaspoon vanilla extract
  2 pears, cored and cut into halves
  ¼ cup granola with almonds

Combine all ingredients, except pears and granola, in slow cooker; mix well. Place pears, cut side down, over pineapple mixture. Cover and cook on LOW 3½ to 4½ hours. Arrange pear halves on serving plates. Spoon pineapple mixture over pear halves. Garnish with granola. *Makes 4 servings*

Nutrients per serving: *Calories: 133, Calories from Fat: 2%, Protein: 1 g, Carbohydrate: 34 g, Cholesterol: 0 mg, Sodium: 3 mg, Fiber: 3 g*
DIETARY EXCHANGES: *2 Fruit*

Pumpkin Custard

 2 eggs, beaten
 1 cup canned pumpkin
½ cup packed brown sugar
½ teaspoon ground ginger
½ teaspoon ground cinnamon
½ teaspoon grated lemon peel
 1 can (12 ounces) evaporated milk
   Additional ground cinnamon

1. Combine eggs, pumpkin, brown sugar, ginger, cinnamon and lemon peel in large bowl. Stir in evaporated milk. Pour mixture into a 1½-quart soufflé dish. Cover tightly with foil.

2. Make foil handles (see page 8). Place soufflé dish in slow cooker. Pour water into slow cooker to come about 1½ inches from top of soufflé dish. Cover and cook on LOW 4 hours.

3. Use foil handles to lift dish from slow cooker. Sprinkle with additional ground cinnamon. Serve warm.

Makes 6 servings

Nutrients per serving: *Calories: 256, Calories from Fat: 20%, Protein: 20 g, Carbohydrate: 32 g, Cholesterol: 52 mg, Sodium: 388 mg, Fiber: 5 g*
DIETARY EXCHANGES: *2 Vegetable, 2 Starch, 2 Lean Meat*

Luscious Pecan Bread Pudding

　　3 cups French bread cubes
　　3 tablespoons chopped pecans, toasted
2¼ cups low-fat milk
　　2 eggs, beaten
　½ cup sugar
　　1 teaspoon vanilla
　¾ teaspoon ground cinnamon, divided
　¾ cup reduced-calorie cranberry juice cocktail
1½ cups frozen pitted tart cherries
　　2 tablespoons sugar substitute

1. Toss bread cubes and pecans in soufflé dish. Combine milk, eggs, sugar, vanilla and ½ teaspoon cinnamon in large bowl. Pour over bread mixture in soufflé dish. Cover tightly with foil. Make foil handles (see page 8). Place soufflé dish in slow cooker. Pour hot water into slow cooker to come about 1½ inches from top of soufflé dish. Cover and cook on LOW 2 to 3 hours.

2. Meanwhile, stir together cranberry juice and remaining ¼ teaspoon cinnamon in small saucepan; stir in frozen cherries. Bring sauce to boil over medium heat, about 5 minutes. Remove from heat. Stir in sugar substitute. Lift dish from slow cooker with foil handles. Serve with cherry sauce. *Makes 6 servings*

Nutrients per serving: *Calories: 238, Calories from Fat: 25%, Protein: 8 g, Carbohydrate: 38 g, Cholesterol: 78 mg, Sodium: 154 mg, Fiber: 2 g*
DIETARY EXCHANGES: *1 Fruit, 1 Starch, 1 Fat*

Luscious Pecan Bread Pudding

HEARTY STEWS

Panama Pork Stew

2 small sweet potatoes, peeled and cut into 2-inch
    pieces (about 12 ounces total)
1 package (10 ounces) frozen corn
1 package (9 ounces) frozen cut green beans
1 cup chopped onion
1¼ pounds lean pork stew meat, cut into 1-inch cubes
1 can (14½ ounces) diced tomatoes
1 to 2 tablespoons chili powder
½ teaspoon salt
½ teaspoon ground coriander

Place potatoes, corn, green beans and onion in slow
cooker. Top with pork. Stir together tomatoes, 1 cup
water, chili powder, salt and coriander in large bowl.
Pour over pork in slow cooker. Cover and cook on LOW
7 to 9 hours. *Makes 6 servings*

Old World Chicken and Vegetables

  1 tablespoon dried oregano leaves
  1 teaspoon salt, divided
  1 teaspoon paprika
½ teaspoon garlic powder
¼ teaspoon black pepper
  2 medium green bell peppers, cut into thin strips
  1 small yellow onion, thinly sliced
  1 cut-up whole chicken (3 pounds)
⅓ cup ketchup
  6 ounces dried uncooked egg noodles

1. In a small bowl, combine oregano, ½ teaspoon salt, paprika, garlic powder and pepper; mix well.

2. Place bell peppers and onion in slow cooker. Top with chicken thighs and legs, sprinkle with half of the oregano mixture, top with chicken breasts. Sprinkle chicken with remaining oregano mixture. Cover and cook on LOW 8 hours or on HIGH 4 hours. Stir in ketchup and ½ teaspoon salt. Just before serving, cook noodles following package directions; drain. Serve chicken pieces and vegetables over noodles.

Makes 4 servings

Middle Eastern Lamb Stew

1½ **pounds lamb stew meat, cubed**
2 **tablespoons all-purpose flour**
1 **tablespoon vegetable oil**
1½ **cups beef broth**
1 **cup chopped onion**
½ **cup chopped carrots**
1 **clove garlic, minced**
1 **tablespoon tomato paste**
½ **teaspoon ground cumin**
½ **teaspoon red pepper flakes**
¼ **teaspoon ground cinnamon**
½ **cup chopped dried apricots**
1 **teaspoon salt**
¼ **teaspoon black pepper**
3 **cups hot cooked noodles**

1. Coat lamb cubes with flour; set aside. Heat oil in large nonstick skillet over medium-high heat until hot. Brown half of lamb and transfer to slow cooker; repeat with remaining lamb. Add broth, onion, carrots, garlic, tomato paste, cumin, red pepper and cinnamon. Cover and cook on LOW 3 hours.

2. Stir in apricots, salt and pepper. Cover and cook on LOW 2 to 3 hours, or until lamb is tender and sauce is thickened. Serve lamb over noodles.

Makes 6 servings

Vegetarian Chili

1 tablespoon vegetable oil
1 cup finely chopped onion
1 cup chopped red bell pepper
2 tablespoons minced jalapeño pepper
1 clove garlic, minced
1 can (28 ounces) crushed tomatoes
1 can (14½ ounces) black beans, rinsed and drained
1 can (14 ounces) garbanzo beans, drained
½ cup canned corn
¼ cup tomato paste
1 teaspoon sugar
1 teaspoon ground cumin
1 teaspoon dried basil leaves
1 teaspoon chili powder
¼ teaspoon black pepper
1 cup shredded Cheddar cheese (optional)

1. Heat oil in large nonstick skillet over medium-high heat until hot. Add chopped onion, bell pepper, jalapeño pepper and garlic; cook and stir 5 minutes or until vegetables are tender.

2. Spoon vegetables into slow cooker. Add remaining ingredients, except cheese, to slow cooker; mix well. Cover and cook on LOW 4 to 5 hours. Garnish with cheese, if desired. *Makes 4 servings*

Vegetarian Chili

Mediterranean Meatball Ratatouille

2 tablespoons olive oil, divided
1 pound mild Italian sausage, casings removed
1 package (8 ounces) sliced mushrooms
1 small eggplant, diced
1 zucchini, diced
½ cup chopped onion
1 clove garlic, minced
1 teaspoon dried oregano leaves
1 teaspoon salt
½ teaspoon black pepper
1 tablespoon tomato paste
2 tomatoes, diced
2 tablespoons chopped fresh basil
1 teaspoon fresh lemon juice

1. Pour 1 tablespoon olive oil to 5-quart slow cooker. Shape sausage into 1-inch balls. Place half the meatballs in slow cooker. Add half the mushrooms, eggplant and zucchini. Add onion, garlic, ½ teaspoon oregano, ½ teaspoon salt and ¼ teaspoon pepper.

2. Add remaining meatballs, mushrooms, eggplant and zucchini. Add remaining oregano, salt and pepper. Top with remaining olive oil. Cover and cook on LOW 6 to 7 hours.

3. Stir in tomato paste and diced tomatoes. Cover and cook on LOW 15 minutes. Stir in basil and lemon; serve.

Makes 6 (1⅔ cups) servings

*Mediterranean Meatball
Ratatouille*

Hearty Chili Mac

 1 pound lean ground beef
 1 can (14½ ounces) diced tomatoes, drained
 1 cup chopped onion
 1 clove garlic, minced
 ½ teaspoon salt
 ½ teaspoon ground cumin
 ½ teaspoon dried oregano leaves
 ¼ teaspoon black pepper
 ¼ teaspoon red pepper flakes
 1 tablespoon chili powder
 2 cups cooked macaroni

Crumble ground beef into slow cooker. Add remaining ingredients, except macaroni, to slow cooker. Cover and cook on LOW 4 hours. Stir in cooked macaroni. Cover and cook on LOW 1 hour. *Makes 4 servings*

Hearty Chili Mac

Chicken and Chili Pepper Stew

1 pound boneless skinless chicken thighs, cut into
½-inch pieces

1 pound small potatoes, cut lengthwise in halves and
then cut crosswise into slices

1 cup chopped onion

2 poblano chili peppers, seeded and cut into ½-inch
pieces

1 jalapeño pepper, seeded and finely chopped

3 cloves garlic, minced

3 cups fat-free reduced-sodium chicken broth

1 can (14½ ounces) no-salt-added diced tomatoes

2 tablespoons chili powder

1 teaspoon dried oregano leaves

1. Place chicken, potatoes, onion, poblano peppers, jalapeño pepper and garlic in slow cooker.

2. Stir together broth, tomatoes, chili powder and oregano in large bowl. Pour broth mixture over chicken mixture in slow cooker. Stir. Cover and cook on LOW 8 to 9 hours. 			*Makes 6 servings*

Picadillo

1 pound ground beef
1 small onion, chopped
1 clove garlic, minced
1 can (16 ounces) diced tomatoes, undrained
¼ cup golden raisins
1 tablespoon chili powder
1 tablespoon cider vinegar
½ teaspoon ground cumin
½ teaspoon dried oregano leaves
½ teaspoon ground cinnamon
¼ teaspoon red pepper flakes
1 teaspoon salt
¼ cup slivered almonds (optional)

Cook ground beef, onion and garlic in medium nonstick skillet over medium heat until beef is no longer pink; drain. Place mixture in slow cooker. Add tomatoes, raisins, chili powder, vinegar, cumin, oregano, cinnamon and red pepper flakes to slow cooker. Cover and cook on LOW 6 to 7 hours. Stir in salt. Garnish with almonds, if desired.

Makes 4 servings

TIP-TOP TATERS

Sweet-Spiced Sweet Potatoes

2 pounds sweet potatoes, peeled and cut into
    ½-inch pieces
¼ cup dark brown sugar, packed
1 teaspoon ground cinnamon
½ teaspoon ground nutmeg
⅛ teaspoon salt
2 tablespoons butter, cut into ⅛-inch pieces
1 teaspoon vanilla extract

Combine all ingredients, except butter and vanilla, in slow cooker; mix well. Cover and cook on LOW 7 hours or cook on HIGH 4 hours. Add butter and vanilla; stir to blend.   *Makes 4 servings*

Garden Potato Casserole

1¼ pounds baking potatoes, unpeeled and sliced
1 small green or red bell pepper, thinly sliced
¼ cup finely chopped yellow onion
½ teaspoon salt
½ teaspoon dried thyme leaves
   Black pepper to taste
2 tablespoons butter, cut into ⅛-inch pieces, divided
1 small yellow squash, thinly sliced
1 cup (4 ounces) shredded sharp Cheddar cheese

1. Place potatoes, bell pepper, onion, salt, thyme, pepper and 1 tablespoon butter in slow cooker; mix well. Layer the squash evenly over all and sprinkle with remaining tablespoon butter. Cover and cook on LOW 7 hours or on HIGH 4 hours.

2. Remove potato mixture to serving platter. Sprinkle with cheese and let stand 2 to 3 minutes or until cheese melts.

Makes 5 servings

Garden Potato Casserole

Blue Cheese Potatoes

2 pounds red potatoes, peeled and cut into
    ½-inch pieces
1¼ cups chopped green onions, divided
1 teaspoon dried basil leaves
2 tablespoons olive oil, divided
½ teaspoon salt
    Black pepper
2 ounces crumbled blue cheese

1. Layer potatoes, 1 cup onions, basil, 1 tablespoon oil, salt and pepper in slow cooker. Cover and cook on LOW 7 hours or on HIGH 4 hours.

2. Gently stir in cheese and remaining 1 tablespoon oil. If slow cooker is on low turn to HIGH and cook an additional 5 minutes to allow flavors to blend. Transfer potatoes to serving platter and top with remaining ¼ cup onions.   *Makes 5 servings*

Slow Roasted Potatoes

16 small new potatoes
3 tablespoons butter, cut into ⅛-inch pieces
1 teaspoon paprika
½ teaspoon salt
¼ teaspoon garlic powder
Black pepper to taste

Combine all ingredients in slow cooker; mix well. Cover and cook on LOW 7 hours or on HIGH 4 hours. Remove potatoes with slotted spoon to serving dish; cover to keep warm. Add 1 to 2 tablespoons water to drippings and stir until well blended. Pour mixture over potatoes.

Makes 3 to 4 servings

HELPFUL HINT

New potatoes are freshly dug young potatoes. They may be any variety, but most often are round reds.

Potato-Crab Chowder

1 cup frozen hash brown potatoes
1 package (10 ounces) frozen corn
¾ cup finely chopped carrots
1 teaspoon dried thyme leaves
¾ teaspoon garlic-pepper seasoning
3 cups fat-fee reduced-sodium chicken broth
½ cup water
1 cup evaporated milk
3 tablespoons cornstarch
½ cup sliced green onions
1 can (6 ounces) crabmeat, drained

1. Place potatoes, corn and carrots in slow cooker. Sprinkle with thyme and garlic-pepper seasoning.

2. Add broth and water. Cover and cook on LOW for 3½ to 4½ hours.

3. Stir together evaporated milk and cornstarch in medium bowl. Stir into slow cooker. Turn temperature to HIGH. Cover and cook 1 hour. Stir in green onions and crabmeat.

Makes 5 servings

Potato-Crab Chowder

Mediterranean Red Potatoes

2 medium red potatoes, cut in half lengthwise then
  crosswise into pieces
⅔ cup fresh or frozen pearl onions
  Nonstick garlic-flavored cooking spray
¾ teaspoon dried Italian seasoning
¼ teaspoon black pepper
1 small tomato, seeded and chopped
2 ounces feta cheese, crumbled
2 tablespoons chopped black olives

1. Place potatoes and onions in a 1½-quart soufflé dish. Spray potatoes and onions with cooking spray; toss to coat. Add Italian seasoning and pepper; mix well. Cover dish tightly with foil.

2. Make foil handles (see page 8). Place soufflé dish in slow cooker. Pour hot water to come about 1½ inches from top of soufflé dish. Cover and cook on LOW 7 to 8 hours.

3. Use foil handles to lift dish from slow cooker. Stir tomato, feta cheese and olives into potato mixture.

Makes 4 servings

*Mediterranean Red
Potatoes*

Ham and Potato Casserole

1½ pounds red potatoes, peeled and sliced
8 ounces thinly sliced ham
2 poblano chili peppers, cut into thin strips
2 tablespoons olive oil
1 tablespoon dried oregano leaves
¼ teaspoon salt
1 cup (4 ounces) shredded Monterey Jack cheese
    with or without hot peppers
2 tablespoons finely chopped cilantro leaves

1. Combine all ingredients, except cheese and cilantro, in slow cooker; mix well. Cover and cook on LOW 7 hours or on HIGH 4 hours.

2. Transfer potato mixture to serving dish and sprinkle with cheese and cilantro. Let stand 3 minutes or until cheese melts. *Makes 6 to 7 servings*

Parmesan Potato Wedges

2 pounds red potatoes, cut into ½-inch wedges
¼ cup finely chopped yellow onion
1½ teaspoons dried oregano leaves
½ teaspoon salt
    Black pepper to taste
2 tablespoons butter, cut into ⅛-inch pieces
¼ cup (1 ounce) grated Parmesan cheese

Layer potatoes, onion, oregano, salt, pepper and butter in slow cooker. Cook on HIGH 4 hours. Transfer potatoes to serving platter and sprinkle with cheese.
Makes 6 servings

Rustic Garlic Mashed Potatoes

2 pounds baking potatoes, unpeeled and cut into
  ½-inch cubes
¼ cup water
2 tablespoons butter, cut in ⅛-inch pieces
1¼ teaspoons salt
½ teaspoon garlic powder
¼ teaspoon black pepper
1 cup milk

Place all ingredients, except milk, in slow cooker; toss to combine. Cover and cook on LOW 7 hours or on HIGH 4 hours. Add milk to slow cooker. Mash potatoes with potato masher or electric mixer until smooth.

Makes 5 servings

HELPFUL HINT

Scrub potatoes with a vegetable brush under warm running water before cooking to remove embedded dirt.

Swiss Cheese Scalloped Potatoes

   2 pounds baking potatoes, peeled and thinly sliced
½ cup finely chopped yellow onion
¼ teaspoon salt
¼ teaspoon ground nutmeg
   3 tablespoons butter, cut into ⅛-inch pieces
½ cup milk
   2 tablespoons all-purpose flour
   3 ounces Swiss cheese slices, torn into small pieces
¼ cup finely chopped green onion (optional)

1. Layer half the potatoes, ¼ cup onion, ⅛ teaspoon salt, ⅛ teaspoon nutmeg and 1 tablespoon butter in slow cooker. Repeat layers. Cover and cook on LOW 7 hours or on HIGH 4 hours. Remove potatoes with slotted spoon to serving dish.

2. Blend milk and flour in small bowl until smooth. Stir mixture into slow cooker. Add cheese; stir to combine. If slow cooker is on LOW, turn to HIGH, cover and cook until slightly thickened, about 10 minutes. Stir. Pour cheese mixture over potatoes and serve. Garnish with chopped green onions, if desired.

Makes 5 to 6 servings

*Swiss Cheese Scalloped
Potatoes*

Desserts, Snacks & More

Red Pepper Relish

2 large red bell peppers, cut into thin strips
1 small Vidalia or other sweet onion, thinly sliced
3 tablespoons cider vinegar
2 tablespoons brown sugar
1 tablespoon vegetable oil
1 tablespoon honey
¼ teaspoon salt
¼ teaspoon dried thyme leaves
¼ teaspoon red pepper flakes
¼ teaspoon black pepper

Combine all ingredients in slow cooker; mix well. Cover and cook on LOW 4 hours.   *Makes 4 servings*

Banana-Rum Custard with Vanilla Wafers

1½ cups milk

  3 eggs

½ cup sugar

  3 tablespoons dark rum or milk

⅛ teaspoon salt

  1 medium banana, sliced ¼-inch thick

15 to 18 vanilla wafers

    Sliced strawberries, raspberries or kiwis for
    garnish (optional)

1. Beat milk, eggs, sugar, rum and salt in medium bowl. Pour into 1-quart casserole. Do not cover.

2. Add rack to 5-quart slow cooker and pour in 1 cup water. Place casserole on rack. Cover and cook on LOW 3½ to 4 hours. Remove casserole from slow cooker. Arrange banana slices and wafers over custard. Garnish with strawberries, raspberries or kiwis, if desired.

Makes 5 servings

*Banana-Rum Custard with
Vanilla Wafers*

Triple Delicious Hot Chocolate

⅓ cup sugar

¼ cup unsweetened cocoa powder

¼ teaspoon salt

3 cups milk, divided

¾ teaspoon vanilla extract

1 cup heavy cream

1 square (1 ounce) bittersweet chocolate

1 square (1 ounce) white chocolate

¾ cup whipped cream

6 teaspoons mini chocolate chips *or* shaved
    bittersweet chocolate

1. Combine sugar, cocoa, salt and ½ cup milk in medium bowl. Beat until smooth. Pour into slow cooker. Add remaining milk and vanilla. Cover and cook on LOW 2 hours.

2. Add cream. Cover and cook on LOW 10 minutes. Stir in bittersweet and white chocolates.

3. Pour hot chocolate into 6 mugs. Top each with 2 tablespoons whipped cream and 1 teaspoon chocolate chips. *Makes 6 servings*

Triple Delicious Hot Chocolate

Curried Snack Mix

3 tablespoons butter
2 tablespoons brown sugar
1½ teaspoons hot curry powder
¼ teaspoon salt
¼ teaspoon ground cumin
2 cups rice squares cereal
1 cup walnut halves
1 cup dried cranberries

Melt butter in large skillet. Add brown sugar, curry powder, salt and cumin; mix well. Add cereal, walnuts and cranberries and stir to coat. Spoon mixture into slow cooker. Cover and cook on LOW 3 hours. Remove cover; cook an additional 30 minutes.

Makes 16 servings

Cherry Rice Pudding

1½ cups milk
1 cup hot cooked rice
3 eggs, beaten
½ cup sugar
¼ cup dried cherries or cranberries
½ teaspoon almond extract
¼ teaspoon salt

Combine all ingredients in large bowl. Pour mixture into greased 1½-quart casserole. Cover with foil. Add rack to 5-quart slow cooker and pour in 1 cup water. Place casserole on rack. Cover and cook on LOW 4 to 5 hours. Remove casserole from slow cooker. Let stand 15 minutes before serving.

Makes 6 servings

Spiced Citrus Tea

4 tea bags
   Peel of 1 orange
4 cups boiling water
3 tablespoons honey
2 cans (6 ounces each) orange-pineapple juice
3 star anise
3 cinnamon sticks
   Strawberries, raspberries or kiwis (optional)

1. Place tea bags and orange peel in slow cooker. Pour in boiling water. Cover and let steep 10 minutes. Discard tea bags and orange peel.

2. Add remaining ingredients to slow cooker. Cover and cook on LOW 3 hours. Garnish with strawberries, raspberries or kiwis, if desired.   *Makes 6 servings*

HELPFUL HINT

Star anise can be found in Asian markets, gourmet shops and in some larger supermarkets.

Chocolate Croissant Pudding

1½ **cups milk**

3 **eggs**

½ **cup sugar**

¼ **cup unsweetened cocoa powder**

½ **teaspoon vanilla**

¼ **teaspoon salt**

2 **plain croissants, cut into 1-inch pieces.**

½ **cup chocolate chips**

¾ **cup whipped cream (optional)**

1. Beat milk, eggs, sugar, cocoa, vanilla and salt in medium bowl.

2. Grease a 1-quart casserole. Layer half the croissants, chocolate chips and half the egg mixture in casserole. Repeat layers with remaining croissants and egg mixture.

3. Add rack to 5-quart slow cooker and pour in 1 cup water. Place casserole on rack. Cover and cook on LOW 3 to 4 hours. Remove casserole from slow cooker. Top each serving with 2 tablespoons whipped cream, if desired. *Makes 6 servings*

Chocolate Croissant Pudding

Index

METRIC CONVERSION CHART

VOLUME MEASUREMENTS (dry)

⅛ teaspoon = 0.5 mL
¼ teaspoon = 1 mL
½ teaspoon = 2 mL
¾ teaspoon = 4 mL
1 teaspoon = 5 mL
1 tablespoon = 15 mL
2 tablespoons = 30 mL
¼ cup = 60 mL
⅓ cup = 75 mL
½ cup = 125 mL
⅔ cup = 150 mL
¾ cup = 175 mL
1 cup = 250 mL
2 cups = 1 pint = 500 mL
3 cups = 750 mL
4 cups = 1 quart = 1 L

VOLUME MEASUREMENTS (fluid)

1 fluid ounce (2 tablespoons) = 30 mL
4 fluid ounces (½ cup) = 125 mL
8 fluid ounces (1 cup) = 250 mL
12 fluid ounces (1½ cups) = 375 mL
16 fluid ounces (2 cups) = 500 mL

WEIGHTS (mass)

½ ounce = 15 g
1 ounce = 30 g
3 ounces = 90 g
4 ounces = 120 g
8 ounces = 225 g
10 ounces = 285 g
12 ounces = 360 g
16 ounces = 1 pound = 450 g

DIMENSIONS

1/16 inch = 2 mm
⅛ inch = 3 mm
¼ inch = 6 mm
½ inch = 1.5 cm
¾ inch = 2 cm
1 inch = 2.5 cm

OVEN TEMPERATURES

250°F = 120°C
275°F = 140°C
300°F = 150°C
325°F = 160°C
350°F = 180°C
375°F = 190°C
400°F = 200°C
425°F = 220°C
450°F = 230°C

BAKING PAN SIZES

Utensil	Size in Inches/Quarts	Metric Volume	Size in Centimeters
Baking or Cake Pan (square or rectangular)	8×8×2	2 L	20×20×5
	9×9×2	2.5 L	23×23×5
	12×8×2	3 L	30×20×5
	13×9×2	3.5 L	33×23×5
Loaf Pan	8×4×3	1.5 L	20×10×7
	9×5×3	2 L	23×13×7
Round Layer Cake Pan	8×1½	1.2 L	20×4
	9×1½	1.5 L	23×4
Pie Plate	8×1¼	750 mL	20×3
	9×1¼	1 L	23×3
Baking Dish or Casserole	1 quart	1 L	—
	1½ quart	1.5 L	—
	2 quart	2 L	—